ប្រជាជនខ្មែរដែលគ្មានតំណសំណាង

Unfortunate Cambodia

Collection of memories from war torn Cambodia

C H R I S T O P H E R S I M

christsim2000@yahoo.com

Copyright © 2017 Christopher Sim

All rights reserved. No part(s) of this book may be reproduced, distributed or transmitted in any form, or by any means, or stored in a database or retrieval systems without prior expressed written permission of the author of this book.

ISBN: 978-1-5356-0814-5

Table of Contents

Preface 1

Unfortunate Cambodian 5

Chapter 1: My Short Biography 7

Chapter 2: Unfortunate Land and People 11

Chapter 3: After Cambodia Became Independent In 1953 16

Chapter 4: America Had a Direct Link In Overthrowing the King 21

Chapter 5: The Result of President Nixon and Dr. Kissinger's Doctrine 35

Chapter 6: Corruption in Cambodia 39

Chapter 7: Securing the Mekong River Under the American Advisor 46

Chapter 8: Trusting the Americans Until the End 52

Chapter 9: Why Did It Take So Long for the Vietnamese to Rescue Cambodia? 60

Chapter 10: To the United Nations and International Press 64

Chapter 11: To the American People 74

Chapter 12: To My Fellow Cambodians 78

Chapter 13: The Big Mistake of the King 88
Chapter 14: To My Neighboring Thailand and Vietnam 91
Chapter 15: My Own Judgment 94
Chapter 16: To Dr. Kissinger and Other People Involved 99
Chapter 17: Special Thanks 103
Chapter 18: To My Readers 108

Preface

After thirty-five years of silence and two trips back to visit my homeland of Cambodia, everything in my brain had changed completely. I saw the changed landscape, the dusty roads, the sick, the elderly, the children, the muddy river, and the abused and exploited from the foreigners and all the scars left by the war.

I remembered when I was a young student lying down in my bedroom and hearing the announcement from the national radio about the coup that toppled Prince Norodom Sihanouk. I asked myself why it had happened to Cambodia, but I knew that a lot of bad things would happen to the Cambodian people because of it. I had a lot of ideas about why it happened, but I didn't know whom I was supposed to stop or tell, and I was not alone. During the early 1950s, the Viet Minh had already tried to take over and terrorize Cambodia once but were kicked out by the multilateral Paris peace accord. Cambodia was lucky that time.

Now I have my chance to tell the world who was involved, who was the butcher, who was the one that provided all the weapons, who trained and indoctrinated the regular Khmer to become the Khmer Rouge, and who doused gasoline on my beloved country of Cambodia and torched it. In this book I'll explain the connection, and who was behind the death of more than two million Cambodians.

So far the world points the finger at the Khmer Rouge alone, but that is not exactly correct, so at the end of this book you, my reader, will be the judge. The persons and countries that committed the crimes and left their fingerprints at the crime scene in Cambodia try to walk away free, but now is my chance to tell the world my story.

In this book the dates and times might not be correct because I am not writing a historical document. I am writing what I saw, what I heard, what I participated in, and what I remembered. At first, I thought I would take this story to my grave, but it hurt too much when I saw my people during my visit and how the neighboring countries kept moving their borders inside Cambodia. If this book becomes a success, I'll use a big chunk of the profits to help the needy and poor Cambodians.

Unfortunate Cambodia

The idea behind this book is not for revenge, or to embarrass or persecute any country, but to beg them to come back, protect our borders, and help rebuild Cambodia. It has been forty years, but nothing has been done, and I ask them to put politics aside and help rebuild schools, hospitals, roads, and public buildings that were destroyed by their weapons, because this war did not belong to Cambodia at all. The war was created by superpower nations, and the blood-thirsty Vietcong neighboring Cambodia.

My story of how this happened lives in the remembrance of more than TWO MILLION lives lost, and in the suffering and the pain of the survivors, including me, caused by the conflict in my once peaceful land.

So I beg all my readers not to use this book to attack my beloved adopted country of America, and especially the citizens of America. From my point of view, they were victims of this conflict, too. I, Christopher Sim, also known as Ung Chun Sim, take full responsibility for the contents of this book. You are my reader, and perhaps you will understand my explanation and be my judge.

I have had no contact with, did not get any ideas from, or have backing by any Cambodian politician.

Christopher Sim

I want to thank my trusted friend Air Commodore Frank Burtt, OBE Royal Australian Air Force (retired) who encouraged me to write this book.
I hope Dr. Kissinger will also read my book.

Unfortunate Cambodian

What drove me to write this book was to reopen the Cambodian case to the world with peaceful purposes only. What happened to Cambodia forty years ago? I can prove to you who the players were behind the loss of more than two million lives, in addition to the pain and suffering of all the surviving Cambodians. The United Nations and the international press have closed their eyes and pretended they did not see or hear anything until now. After the signing of the peace treaty between the United States and North Vietnam in Paris, both Dr. Kissinger and Le Duc Tho received the Nobel Peace Prize. In addition, the whole world cheered them on.

Now it is my chance. I ask all of you, my readers, to rethink whether Dr. Kissinger and Le Duc Tho were the real peacemakers, or whether they were war criminals? And you might be surprised at who had witnessed the killing field during Pol Pot's regime.

I wrote this book from my heart, not for money, but for the dignity and pride of my people, who were destroyed by the superpowers—the Chinese, Americans, and Russians—and the blood-thirsty Vietcong. We are native to our land since the first century "Funan." The consequences, conspiracies, and hypocrisies of this modern world nearly sent us back to the Stone Age. This book will serve as an X-ray machine to see through the hidden minds of these people and the superpowers.

After you finish reading this book, you will be my judge. We cannot go back and change the past, but we can prevent the future from repeating it. Thank you. Please leave your comments if you wish.

Chapter 1
My Short Biography

My name is Christopher Sim, also known as Ung Chun Sim. I was born during the last year of World War II to a successful businessman named Kaing Siv Heng and his wife Ung Van in Siem Reap in Cambodia, most noted as the location of the Angkor Wat temple. I was the ninth of thirteen children. I spent three years at Lycee Sisovat in Phnom Penh, Cambodia, from 1964 to 1967, and I continued my studies at ITSAK, an institute of technology that was donated by the Soviet Union and taught by Soviet professors, in the capital of Phnom Penh to pursue a career as an electrical engineer.

The house was built by the French governor during World War II and later bought by my parents, where I spent my childhood.
PURSAT, CAMBODIA

When the unexpected war started in early 1970, my classmates were divided, not in terms of politics but in the ways they chose to survive this ordeal. We knew the consequence of the war as we had witnessed and understood the suffering of the Vietnamese and Laotian civilians for decades. I had previous experience with the Vietminh, the predecessor of the Vietcong, when I was a child and that experience will haunt me for the rest of my life. I will elaborate on this in another chapter.

Half of my classmates preferred to remain on the sidelines by continuing their studies, while the rest chose to join the armed forces that were backed by the United States to fight the invader, the Vietcong. I decided to join the Khmer Air Force "8." At first, I was trained to become an army officer at Ecole Militaire Khmer. The school was half funded and trained by the French officers and French government in Phnom Penh. I was later selected to go to Australia to train as a pilot by the Royal Australian Air Force (RAAF) "No. 15 Army Pilot Course" at Point Cook, Victoria, Australia. There I met my wonderful course supervisor SQDR F.W. Burtt, his wife, and his two brilliant daughters. They were all to become my trusted friends.

After I went back to Cambodia, I was assigned to join the forward air control squadron. I flew the Helio AU-24 Stallion gunship with close ground support on day and night missions until almost three months before the end of the war. The Cambodian staff sent me to Thailand to become an instrument procedure instructor with the US military assistant command in Thailand. I graduated at the same time the war ended on April 17, 1975. I became a refugee and received asylum in the United States, and settled down in California. I was a mail carrier for the United States Postal Service for over thirty years and retired in

2012. I am married with two daughters and a son, all of them graduated.

At the end of the war I found only three of my classmates still alive so far.

Graduation as instrument instructor pilot in 1975. UDORN, THAILAND

Chapter 2
Unfortunate Land and People

Cambodia is located between overpopulated Thailand and Vietnam. For the past eight hundred years, Cambodia has had two enemies, one to the east and another to the west. In the early 1800s, Cambodians were nearly wiped out. Luckily, the French came to the rescue Cambodia. Thailand had already taken the two northwestern provinces, Siem Reap and Battambang. The French forces reclaimed both for Cambodia. During World War II, Cambodia was invaded by the Japanese, who attempted to use us as a stepping stone to invade Thailand, but by then the war had ended.

At the time, I was still in my mother's womb. When I was big enough to understand, she told me a story. My parents had left Phnom Penh by boat along the Tonlé Sap, a river that connects the capital to a big lake. The war had already ended, the Japanese had surrendered, and the Cambodians, including my mother and father, attempted to resume their normal lives. However, when the French took control, two planes flew over her head and shockingly dropped bombs in the heart of the capital, Phsar Kendal market, killing and injuring hundreds of civilians. All the Cambodians who know this story are still scratching their heads. We do not know who did it and why they did it, but this is only the beginning of my story.

During the late 1940s, my father was a fish farmer and catcher. He employed fifty to over a hundred employees depending on the season. We moved from place to place during the dry season, and we built a temporary house in the middle of the lake. At that time, Cambodia's countryside was controlled by three factions: the French, the Cambodian liberation front(Eksarak), and the Vietnamese communist—Vietminh—invader. The Cambodian liberation front, to my knowledge, only received support from the Cambodians, but they fought both fronts with the French and the Vietminh, the predecessor of the Vietcong. Somehow, my father, who was a brilliant man, managed to get along with all of them.

One day during my childhood, while my family was temporarily living on a boat in a small village by the western shore of Tonlé Sap named Reang Til in the province of Pursat, there was a surprise visit by two armed men. They were dressed in black with small white stripes, and carrying two rifles. They spoke Vietnamese with my father. I later discovered that they were high ranking Vietminh and were demanding my father hand over one of his handsome employees to them. Later the same day, I heard a loud single gunshot. I was shaking and so frightened, I felt like I was going to throw up. I cried, and my mother hugged me and said, "They're not going to hurt us, son."

They killed him and buried him in a very shallow ditch, allowing the wild animals to take care of the rest. His body was left at the side of a single dirt trail that linked the floating village to the only pagoda of that small village to make sure all the villagers saw it. The whole village was scared to death and left wondering who would be next. At that time I was a rich, spoiled child and I only allowed some of my father's employees to hold me. The man who was executed was my best friend, and he was one of them. They wrongly accused him of being a spy for the French. At the time, less than 5% of the employees were able to read or write. The Vietminh executed him because of the way he looked and his ability to read. After almost sixty years, I am finally able to put the unjust execution of one of my most peaceful, innocent friends to rest, but it still haunts me.

As I got older, I came to fully understand that this was a classic tactic of intimidation for the Vietnamese communists. When they invaded Cambodia's countryside, civilians were forced to comply or face execution. They came with bayonets, cannons, and rockets, not with flowers in their hands. There was a lot of innocent blood shed during their passage through. In 1979, the Vietnamese communists kicked the Khmer Rouge out of power and mainly kept hunting down all Khmer patriotic too. The first wave of Cambodian refugees included ill individuals, orphans, elders, women, and children, all of whom survived starvation and persecution, crossed the Thai border to seek temporary refuge in Thailand.

During that time, there was a slow response from the United Nations, and somehow, the Thai government rounded them up and dumped them along the Thai border, in Phnom Dong Rek mountains range, to make sure they did not come back again. The Thai soldiers blasted them from behind with machine guns and the 105 mm howitzer. There was a lot of blood spilled from the suffering of Cambodian refugees. This part, I still don't understand until now. The whole world, including

Unfortunate Cambodia

the international press and the United Nations themselves, failed to criticize the Thai Government for its actions. I do not want to compare this action to Hitler, but you'll be the judge.

Amberley air base, Queensland, Australia - 1973

Chapter 3
After Cambodia Became Independent In 1953

After becoming independent in 1953 during my childhood, Cambodia became a peaceful land again. The Khmer revolution fighter (Eksarak), as I mentioned in previous chapter, was now dissolved and later joined the government that was ruled by King Norodom Sihanouk. In addition to the changes that occurred within the country, a multilateral peace accord kicked the Vietminh out of Cambodia.

It was the first time the United States and Cambodia exchanged ambassadors. America provided us with minimal amounts of education, healthcare, finances, and military. The Cambodians loved it. I remembered following the American library "van wagon," which traveled through the countryside of Cambodia by wheel, to get a free monthly magazine written in Cambodian titled *Lork Serey (Free World)*. Each month, the children in the countryside waited for the library to arrive—that was

Unfortunate Cambodia

the only free luxury they could look forward to. They showed us cartoons, educational films, and health reports, and gave us free magazines, entertainment, and live music performed by American musicians. It is still very emotional for me when I look back and remember the love Cambodian kids gad toward America at that time.

During that same year, the United Nations (UN) divided Vietnam in two—the north belonging to the communists, and the south belonging to a republic. However, the Vietminh refused to leave the south, and they renamed themselves the Vietcong to get around the Geneva Convention. The French then left Vietnam and the United States moved in, not to fight but to assist and advise the South Vietnamese forces to protect their freedom. That was how the Vietnam War escalated.

In the early 1960s, Cambodia was an oasis of peace with four million Cambodians proving themselves to be self-sufficient. They had skills and resources while having the freedom to travel with no restrictions. The crime rate was extremely low. Inflation was minimal, and with a little money, citizens could purchase plenty of food and produce. There were no communists, but neighboring Vietnam was inflamed. The Vietcong left Cambodia alone, but the tension between the two countries was comparable to a game of cat and mouse.

Deaths, bombings, and heavy fighting were on the rise in Vietnam with no end in sight. On the Cambodian side, the king spent most of his budget on free education and heath care, which made him very popular with his people, including the young and especially the extremely impoverished. That gave the communists a very hard time in infiltrating and taking over Cambodia.

Cambodia, when ruled by the king, was accustomed to the luxuries of free education, healthcare, and freedom, among other things. If one were to actually analyze and understand the king's policies, one would realize that the king was, in fact, helping the West protect Cambodia's freedom against the advancing communists. However, the Americans did not see it that way, and tragically both the Vietcong and the Americans wanted to use Cambodia as a steppingstone.

All the high-ranking leaders of the Khmer Rouge—Hou Yon, Hou Nim, Ierng Sary, Kheo Samphan, Norng Suon, Chuon Mom, Chuon Choeun, Earng Sary, Pol Pot—were under guard or house arrest by the king's secret police. The CIA knew it, too. Sometimes the king's secret police secretly killed some of them, but not enough to please the US State Department and Dr. Kissinger. Tragically, the Vietcong had already planned to invade and take over Cambodia, but were waiting for the Americans to start first. The Americans knew exactly when to start the fire by using Lon Nol and Prince Sirik Matak to take down the king.

Many people would ask the question, How did Cambodia remain at peace for so long? During that time Cambodia had very few armed forces, only around 20,000 men including the police forces. Because of this, it was as though we were all in a small, fragile boat that was directed by the king between two powerful hurricanes—the Vietcong and the United States. In my opinion, if the King had joined the Americans, the Vietcong would have moved into Cambodia without hesitation. I believed he was a great politician at the time and played the right card by proclaiming Cambodia a neutral country. In exchange for peace with the communists, he showed sympathy toward them, and condemned all American actions toward Vietnam.

Unfortunately, this was a dangerous move against the Americans, but was the only acceptable option on the table for the king. His job was to provide harmony, happiness, prosperity, and peace to his six million people without firing a shot or losing land. His policies had worked for number of years, but now the king, with his policies, had to face the richest and the most powerful country on earth, the United States.

Strategically, Cambodia is located between Thailand and Vietnam. All of American's most sophisticated fighters and bombers, including B-52s, were based in Thailand. The Americans badly needed Cambodian airspace to conduct business in Vietnam, and then return to their base in Thailand without going around Cambodia. If Cambodia got involved, the Americans could finally bomb any target in Cambodia with no restrictions. It got to the point where Dr. Kissinger, and President Richard Nixon and his advisors, felt they had to push Cambodia into the war at any cost. President Nixon and Dr. Kissinger had a few options, but picked one that caused the loss of more than two millions lives, plus pain and suffering for many others. My in-depth explanation is in another chapter.

Chapter 4
America Had a Direct Link In Overthrowing the King

After Cambodia became independent, the United States and Cambodia were initially very friendly. However, during the late 1950s, the Americans played two roles by creating and financing one of the rebellion forces—the Khmer Serey, located on the Thai border on the ridge of the Phnom Dang Rek mountain range. The CIA equipped them with small arms and a radio broadcast called the *Voice of Freedom*. They were led by Son Ngoc Thanh. Their intention was to overthrow the king. It was a very unpopular action among Cambodians, but the CIA did it anyway. The discomfort, hate, and anger toward American policies grew. I still remember one peaceful evening when I heard a loud explosion from the direction of the royal palace. We later found out in the news that somebody tried to kill the king and his family with a bomb planted inside a gift. Luckily, the king's family escaped. One year later, the international press detected and published the entire letter that linked the CIA and the Khmer rebellion to the bombing, but the State Department denied that. I actually read the letter in one of the Cambodian newspapers that had translated it into the Khmer language.

A few years later, in the late 1950s, there was another coup. This time the governor of the province of Siem Reap, Dab Chhuon, got involved. The CIA provided him with radio access, printed money, and 250 kg of solid gold bars, and tried to proclaim his province as independent from the kingdom. The population at that time was strongly behind the king. The king discovered the plan just two days before and rounded up the opposition and executed them all, including two foreigners who refused to talk. The most important factor in this was that Dab Chhuon was captured and killed by ordinary citizens. The king had gotten to the point that he could not take American policy anymore. He kicked the Americans out entirely and refused any kind of aid. The Americans were shocked. American senator Mike Mansfield's trusted friend Norodom Sihanouk tried to reverse his decision, but failed. The Chinese and Russians now began taking over by providing aid to Cambodia.

Unfortunate Cambodia

Years later, I heard a rumor that the king had allowed weapons and medicine to flow through Cambodia and into the hands of the Vietcong in South Vietnam. I agreed with that, but only on a very small scale despite the fact that I did not witness it. Cambodia, at that time, was a free country because of this. The CIA knew exactly how much it was.

There was only one main highway, No. 4, which linked Sihanouk Ville, the only seaport, to the capital. I heard from the news that some American congressmen had made demands to bomb that seaport, but the State Department preferred a different way to solve the problem. At the same time, the State Department accused the king of allowing the Vietcong to build hospitals along the border and use them as shelters. Imagine, the Cambodians had 20,000 armed men, including the police forces—how were we to stop the war machine, the blood-thirsty Vietcong? Regardless of whether or not the king gave his permission, they did it anyway. However, they still gave us peace by not to invading our country. In contrast, if we look at the American side, think of this—the Americans and allied forces, ground and air, crossed into Cambodia as many times as they wanted but in secret, and they even dropped bombs inside Cambodia killing innocent people.

Over the past decade the Americans tried to get rid of Prince Norodom Sihanouk, but failed. This time, it worked by using Lon Nol, army chief of staff; Prince Sirik Matak, a cousin of the king; his gangs; the Cambodian congressmen; and some senators. It was unconstitutional. Actually, Lon Nol's gun was pointed at the back of these people.

After the coup, the townspeople were very upset but kept quiet. The countryside and the poorest of the poor started to express their anger, though, looking to bring the king back. They did not have any weapons, only knives and fists. At first, they turned to violence that was out of control. They killed one of Lon Nol's brothers, a small-town governor, and later, only with their knives and fists, killed two more congressmen in the province of Kampong Cham. Then, the crowd headed toward the capital along highway No. 1 that linked Phnom Penh to Saigon, but this time they were blocked by tanks with 50 caliber machine guns. With no hesitation, the army opened fire on the unarmed men. Nobody knew how many people died or were injured, but the crowd promised to come back next time with guns.

The Vietcong, who were on the sidelines for more than a decade, now took advantage of the opportunity to invade the peaceful land. They promised to push the

Unfortunate Cambodia

Americans back, as well as the government ruled by Lon Nol, to bring the king back. Unfortunately, despite their promises, the Vietcong wanted nothing else but to turn Cambodia into a communist country and colonize it. To confuse the people in the countryside, the first wave of Vietcong that invaded Cambodia wore a picture of the king on their uniforms.

The Americans now had access to the airspace and ground of Southeast Asia, including Cambodia. Did anybody remember Nixon's doctrine? During a speech given while he was in power, President Nixon gave the green light to bomb Cambodia six months before telling Congress. At first the CIA backed the government for removing their beloved king, the one that gave the people happiness, prosperity, pride, dignity, free education, healthcare, and relative peace in the region. We were not rich before the war, but we had plenty of food to feed our population. Some of the farmers worked only six months out of the year, and were accustomed to a vacation for the next six months while waiting for the rainy season to come. However, Dr. Kissinger, his advisors, and the blood-thirsty Vietcong kept stalking us nonstop until they succeeded. During the next five years, the people in the countryside received bombs, rockets, napalm, and even a B-52 raid without doing any assessment on the ground.

Now, I invite all of you, my readers, to walk on the path of the Cambodians who were trapped or cut off from civilization by the first wave of Vietcong communists. In less than four weeks, they controlled and occupied 80% of the country, including all the northeastern provinces (Preah Vihear, Kratié, Stoeung Treng, Ratanakiri, and Mondulkiri) that linked Cambodia to Laos and South Vietnam. All of these provinces now belonged to the US Air Force. The Cambodian Air Force did not have any long-range aircraft to fly that far without refueling.

The people were trapped behind enemy lines. At first, they were not communists at all. They loved, and were accustomed to freedom and peace. During the first three months of fighting, one of our pilots, Major Ma Kim Oeun, crashed his T-28 in a territory controlled by the Vietcong. An ordinary Cambodian citizen gave him clothing and helped hide him from the Vietcong until the rescue units came. After that, nobody knew the fate of the helper. In this instance, I wanted to prove that the poor people of the countryside were friendly to us from the beginning, even to the pilot who dropped bombs to burn down their village.

Some of the people trapped behind enemy lines included citizens who were well-educated

Unfortunate Cambodia

professionals, while others had large families who could not afford to move to a big town, specifically those who were the poorest of the poor. They preferred to stay where they belonged. They had farmed and raised cattle in some places for generations. Most of them loved the king. Now, the communist, Vietcong were tightening their screws on them. These poor farmers were risking their lives by choosing between their beloved king and the communist regime. At that time, I did not know or understand how we did not have any refugee camps. Maybe the United Nations did not like Lon Nol's government and the Americans. In addition, the Americans only concentrated on bullets and bombs, not the social problems that were created by them.

For the next five years the country people received nothing from Lon Nol's government, or aid from the United States other than bombs. Now the American Air Force could strike any target they wanted inside Cambodia. The first wave of precision dive-bombing from the Americans targeted all the vacation homes and resorts that were owned by the king. I did not understand this strategy, or the hatred toward the king. They targeted public buildings, large hospitals, and pagodas, among many other structures. I knew the communist Vietcong were not stupid enough to use these types of luxury facilities as their resting places. If you, my reader, visit Cambodia now, you might still see scars left from these attacks in Pich Nil, Kirirom, Kg. Sela, Bokor, Yaklom, Sambo Prey Kuk, and even downtown Stoeung Treng province. Then you could imagine how the country people felt.

All the schools, hospitals, and public buildings were closed, destroyed, or burned out by the bombing. Public workers, teachers, and nurses no longer had salaries. Hospitals didn't have doctors. Pharmacies didn't have medicine. The markets didn't have activity. Imagine the carpet-bombings by the B-52s that raided the countryside. Ninety-five percent of the victims were innocent people that included women, children, pregnant women, the elderly, and babies. Entire families were wiped out while they were asleep if the attacks occurred in the evening. A small infection from the blast could become a painful death, a single drop of liquid from napalm could burn human flesh to the bone, and there were no hospitals or surgeons.

We bombed bridges into the cities, moving trucks, boats carrying produce, rice fields, even the pagodas. The pain suffered from the loss of their loved ones persuaded the survivors to fight side by side with the Vietcong. A young child who endured suffering did not care about the king anymore. Little by little, they grew to become the hardcore Khmer Rouge. The Vietcong began reaching their ultimate goal. From the hardcore communist group, the Khmer Rouge was born.

During peaceful years, many children from poor families were kidnapped from Cambodia and ended up in Hanoi to be trained and indoctrinated by the communist Vietcong. They were well prepared for this conflict. When the Vietcong invaded Cambodia, they brought with them this psychological weapon. They spoke fluent Khmer and Vietnamese, but their minds were no longer Cambodian. These young men were ordered to fight Lon Nol's government, whose regime was backed by the American government.

Remember, this entire Vietcong invasion was funded by the Chinese and Russians. All the rockets, 122mm guns, RPGs, AK-47s, cannons, machine guns, hand grenades, and land mines were provided by the Chinese and Russians, and were responsible for the deaths and injuries of innocent people. Without the funds, supplies, and weapons, the Vietcong had nothing but teeth and fingernails to serve as weapons. The innocent people on both sides of the battle, the ones who lived in towns and the ones who lived in the countryside, suffered because of this. And they became great enemies to each other. Dr. Kissinger and President Nixon's plan worked perfectly, but the expected outcome failed completely. I will explain this further later.

Just a couple days after the coup, Lon Nol's government had a lot of money to recruit soldiers. At that time, Cambodia was broke, so where did the money come from? Air America (run by the CIA) landed at night at Pochentong International Airport every hour, and brought with them a lot of small arms, some used while some of them were new, but there was nothing advanced, like an AR-15.

Remember, less than a month after the coup, the American Congress rushed to give military aid to Lon Nol's government. WHY? During that time, Cambodia had already lost 80% of its country to the invaders, the Vietcong. The South Vietnamese navy helped patrol and secure territory along the Mekong River from the border all the way to Phnom Penh, the capital, for ensure the flow of supplies. I fully understood that the great Americans, at this time, intended to fight and protect freedom around the world. However, in this case, the CIA, along with Dr. Kissinger and President Nixon, took freedom away from the peaceful six million Cambodians, the poorest of the poor, without giving them a chance to

Unfortunate Cambodia

vote for a referendum. We had produced the food on our table, and then our food was brought to us by ship and through American aid.

Think of this—if there was no military aid, no heavy bombing, no money, and no assistance from the United States and the American allied forces, the Vietcong would have taken over Cambodia and turned into a communist country in less than sixty days without a doubt. Here is the good part—these six million Cambodians would have mostly remained loyal to the king. Of course the Vietcong would not have given Cambodia back to the king, but they could not have killed millions of us, either. More than two million lives could have been spared because the hard-core Khmer Rouge did not yet exist. But this was not in Kissinger and President Nixon's doctrine. The doctrine wanted the Cambodian to go to war, including people like me.

AND NOW, HERE IS THE BALL GAME. Kissinger and Nixon knew that when they chose to remove the king, the Vietcong would invade Cambodia. They also understood that the Cambodian people hated the Vietcong and would have to protect their land by going to war. When they finally chose to go to war, they would need the Americans help, and the Americans would give them military aid, regardless if the Cambodians needed it or not. Dr. Kissinger and the president intended to open another war front with six million Cambodians, including the elderly, women, and children in front of them. All the Americans had to do was give Cambodians the bullets, bombs, cheap food, cheap uniforms, and a little money. Some of the weapons provided resembled caveman-like tools at the beginning of the war. This way, Kissinger did not need to put American boots on the ground. I, Christopher Sim, even at a very young age, fully understood Kissinger's plan. He thought he could weaken the strength of the Vietcong to make them fight two fronts, and then he would be able to bring them to the table for peace negotiations, allowing the Americans to walk out of Southeast Asia without losing face. His other intention was to bring Cambodia to its knees.

For the next five years, until the fall of Lon Nol's government, American taxpayers controlled the pulse, the blood pressure, the food supply, the armaments, the airplanes, and the bombs. Imagine, in less than sixty days, the CIA, Dr. Kissinger, and President Nixon turned a peaceful land with six million Cambodians upside down. The plan worked perfectly, but the result failed completely. I will explain in my later as I have not yet addressed the consequences at this point.

Along with most of the surviving Cambodians, I hated both the American policy at that time and the Vietcong, but what could we do? We could either sit on the sidelines, join the Vietcong, help to form the Khmer Rouge, or join hands with Lon Nol, who was backed by the United States to fight the Vietcong invaders.

Most of the Cambodians at that time, including students, the rich and poor, and me, did not have any options left. We felt as though we were being pushed from behind by the United States all the way to the bottom of the Grand Canyon, unable to climb back to the rim. We made the only decision that we will never regret by voluntarily letting the Americans carry us the way they wanted to with no ending in sight, even eventually to the death. Now you, my readers, understand why thousands of young Cambodian students joined the Cambodian armed forces at that time, including myself. We hated the war, but we had to go to war to survive. At first, the world looked at us like we were fools. And now, here is the truth that has been silenced for over fifty years.

During the first three months, Lon Nol's regime cowardly executed two of its own senior officers. One of them, Colonel Seng Sun Thai, was killed by Lon

Nol's secret police because he refused to cooperate. It was only a quarter of a mile from where I used to live. Colonel Tom Saravan was executed by his death squad. He was a highly educated and decorated man of honor during the fight with the Vietminh, and was well known as a mastermind behind the plan to seize Prasat Preah Vihear from the Thai. He was a great and brilliant hero to his subordinates by refusing the order to hold the position and fight to the death with only his caveman-like tools against the blood-thirsty Vietcong. He actually saved a lot of lives under his command. May his soul live in peace.

Receiving my wing during graduation at Amberley Air Base, 1973.

Chapter 5
The Result of President Nixon and Dr. Kissinger's Doctrine

Dr. Kissinger opened another chapter of war in his grand scheme by making Cambodia go to war. Now the Vietcong had to fight two fronts—the war in Cambodia, which was fought to spread communism, and the ongoing battle with the South Vietnamese forces, which was backed by the Americans. He expected to weaken the strength of the Vietcong and to bring them to a peaceful negotiation. The Americans were frustrated with the war, with the increasing deaths, and with the politics occurring at home and around the world. There was simply no easy way out. After the Cambodians got involved in the war, nothing could help the American and the South Vietnamese forces. The number of battles, deaths, and injured were on the rise. Up to this point in the war, their plan was perfectly executed, but now their strategy failed completely.

Everyone knew the Americans could have won that war easily, but they did not want to. America had all the tools and technology to win. From the beginning of the war to the time the Americans finally made the decision to pull out, they did not bomb Hai Phong, the largest seaport that brought all the heavy arms and equipment to the Vietcong from China and Russia.

Does anybody really know what brought the Vietcong to the peace talks in Paris? The Americans chose to establish themselves deep inside North Vietnam territory and choke the vital systems of the Vietcong. Finally, they bombed Hai Phong, and only a few miles from the heart of Hanoi. Does anybody remember how many times Le Duc Tho walked out of the peace talks because the Americans temporarily halted the bombing? Every time the Americans did that, the North Vietnamese rebuilt their air defense systems. In the end, the Americans brought Le Duc Tho to his knees by bombing nonstop. Soon after, the peace treaty was signed, the POWs were released, and the American troops withdrew. All these events did not result from Cambodia entering the war.

From that moment on, the consequences of their doctrine virtually destroyed Cambodia and created all kinds of suffering for six millions Cambodians, including the loss of approximately two million lives. To make matters worse, the whole world cheered and praised the two politicians by awarding Dr. Kissinger and Le Duc Tho the most prestigious award on earth, the Nobel Peace Prize. Both of them received the award with smiles and laughter while their hands were covered in Cambodia's blood. In writing this, I had to take a long break from my computer. I have no tears to cry at this time, and I have swallowed my pain as much as I could. I will one day take these painful memories to my grave like the rest of living Cambodians.

We are Cambodians, and while 90% of us still practice Buddhism, including myself, I believe from my own thoughts that Christ, and only Christ, will understand these premeditated actions made by Dr. Kissinger, Le Duc Tho, and the Vietnamese Vietcong. Please do not think that I have overlooked Pol Pot's regime. You will hear from me in an upcoming chapter.

Kissinger and Nixon already had plans for peace talks with the Vietcong to withdraw American troops from Vietnam. Why didn't they leave Cambodia alone? If they had left Cambodia alone, Cambodia would have had a very good chance to survive the takeover by the communists at the end of the Vietnam

War, and more than two millions lives could have been spared.

The communist Vietcong couldn't have infiltrated Cambodia as long as the king was still in power because the King had a lot of very good and trusted leaders by his side from the Eastern & western bloc such as Mr. Charles De Gaulle, the president of France. Make note that the king and his regime had kicked the communist Vietminh out of Cambodia in 1953. The king and his genius politics provided six million Cambodians with peace, prosperity, happiness, free education, and healthcare. And not just that, he led his country to stand face to face with both the most powerful country on earth, the United States, and the blood-thirsty Vietcong without firing a shot or losing land for more than a decade.

Chapter 6
Corruption in Cambodia

Before the coup, Cambodia was self-sufficient in food production. In some cases, we exported food to the neighboring countries and to Singapore on a small scale, specifically dried fish from Tonlé Sap. After the coup, only 25% to 30% of our land and water was controlled by Cambodian forces, even after having large support from the American and South Vietnamese forces. We produced less and less food for the people, and Cambodians were in dire need of more and more aid that included everyday items, plus all kinds of necessities donated by the American taxpayer. I did not know how Nixon and Kissinger were preparing for these consequences.

Now we were floating in the river at the bottom of the Grand Canyon, looking up to the rim and waiting for food and bullets just to survive another day and to fight for the next. The most painful outcome of the war was that Cambodian soldiers were being put under the large microscope of the American media and State Department. They blamed us for everything, from misuse of equipment to wasting and stealing American taxpayer money. They thought we did not fight hard enough to win the war. The American media reported biased images and information to Congress and the American people. American newspaper and television reporters were everywhere, and they only told the story that they wanted to tell. I agreed with some reporting of the corruption during the war. Now is my chance to turn the microscope around and look back at the America side.

I prefer to compare Cambodia at that time to a healthy human being who had fallen victim to Dr. Kissinger holding a syringe filled with a deadly virus, the Vietcong, and secretly injecting it into the unassuming patient. When the deadly virus invaded and transformed into an incurable disease, he gave only medicine to prolong the patient's life to fight against the virus but not to cure. This way, Dr. Kissinger could control or end the patient's life any time he wanted to. His strategy was to make it look like a normal infection. His tactics were successful, because the whole world and the international press, up until now, still considers the war in Cambodia to be a civil war. Of course, each of them has two eyes, one eye closed and the other eye looking in a different direction.

Cambodia could not go to war and win with bullets and bombs alone. We sent our soldiers to die on the battlefield to keep the communists from moving rapidly to the west, and to fulfill Kissinger and Nixon's doctrine, but we did not have enough money to take care of our loved ones who were left behind. The morale of the soldiers was actually very low.

Before the war, the average salary of a high school teacher was $150 to $200 per month. They had a comfortable life at that time. Some of them were able to own property and even luxuries. When the war started, the Cambodian government still used the Cambodian riel as the main currency to pay public workers, teachers, soldiers, and nurses. When the war went into its second phase, inflation went up 100 times 100% (10,000%). Salaries in Cambodian money could not keep up with inflation. Economic aid from the Unites States could solve only a small part of the problem. That is why at that time, many teachers and public workers took time off from work or refused to go to work. They were now unable to feed their families and were looking for alternative income. On the military side, everybody tried to survive by doing anything to feed themselves and their families at home. As a pilot flying a gunship, I got paid 25,000 riels ($10.00) a month, but I still felt more fortunate than the soldiers who got paid only $5.00 a month. That is how the corruption started. I do not blame the American taxpayer at all. I know they did not want to see the people in Cambodia "stealing" their hard-earned money. They were victimized in this conflict just like the Cambodian people were. They did not open this new chapter of war, but they were forced to obey American laws.

The American taxpayer and Congress never asked or understood the life of Cambodians before the war—why the soldiers stole, how the war was started, why it took so long to start the Cambodian war, why the communists did not take over Cambodia a long time ago, or when the king was in actually in power. It was nearly the end of the Vietnam War, just months before the pullout of American troops from Vietnam. They did not know when we went to fight the communists, and if we died, not to do so with an empty stomach. The war itself actually did not belong to us at all. Kissinger, Nixon, and the CIA orchestrated it.

When Dr. Kissinger and the CIA secretly started the fire in Cambodia, they did not ask Congress or the public for permission. However, when it came to aid to Cambodia, they answered "YES." Of the aid that Americans gave to us, most of it went to military hardware. They did not fix the social problems that were caused by the war because nobody brought real news into the living rooms of the American people. I do not have any hard evidence to prove this to you, only logic. I apologize if my thinking is too radical, but this is only a book.

The theft of aid to Cambodia at that time was done mostly by the Americans themselves. American suppliers, entrepreneurs, and middlemen could easily jack up the price of bullets, bombs, tanks, airplanes, spare parts, navy boats, and anything else. The Cambodian government had no right to bargain for prices, only to accept them. The cost of B-52 raids in the countryside, the precision dive bombers, the observer planes, and the leisurely trips of American high ranking officers who flew over Cambodia to Thailand were all expenses that were deducted from American aid. Nothing was free, which is why the bottom line but $10.00 a month, cheap food, cheap uniforms and bullets to fight to death. The auditors, accountants, and people who did the billing were all Americans, and the Cambodian government had to sign and accept. Actually, there was nothing much left to steal during and after the war. Not a single surviving high-ranking Cambodian became rich, or came close to becoming a millionaire, from stealing American money. Six million Cambodians were trapped by Kissinger and Nixon's doctrine with no way out.

At this time, the job of commander or platoon leader was not only to fight the Khmer Rouge and Vietcong, but also to help solve the social problems of soldiers under their command. They lived with the families of soldiers, including their babies. Some of their assignments included DEFENDING SMALL TOWNS. The painful part was that during the Khmer Rouge and Vietcong's hustle to take over small towns, the wives of soldiers helped reload guns for their husbands until the last bullet, or their last drop of blood, was gone. They were not on the payroll and American advisors knew it, which is why when the communists won they executed everybody in the soldier's family. These families could use the extra cash in Cambodian money from stealing to solve most of the problems and needs of their families, ranging from medicine to baby milk.

On the American side these actions were seen as criminal, but to the families of these soldiers and me, their commanders were their only God. I took part in these actions several times. When I landed my plane in any town outside of the capital, I always conducted some kind of business just to earn cash for food. Sometimes I unlawfully used my plane to carry produce into the capital, but only at the end of a mission and when the plane was empty. One time I ran into an American official (I called him SUNNY) and instead of reporting me to my commander, he helped me carry all the merchandise to the market in his SUV that had a diplomatic license plate. We became friends, and he fully understood our tough life with only $10.00 a month in salary to fight a war with no ending in sight. I will never forget his gratitude, and understanding my tough life until the day I die. The State Department is so smart—they never, ever sent a cardboard box filled with American dollars to the Cambodian government, only cheap food, bullets, and printed Cambodian money.

Chapter 7
**Securing the Mekong River
Under the American Advisor**

Five months before Cambodia had fallen into the hands of the Khmer Rouge, American military and economic aid got smaller and smaller, and the offense of the Khmer Rouge got stronger and stronger. Town by town fell into the hands of the Khmer Rouge. The dry season was coming. The Khmer Rouge tried to zero in on the capital. At first, they increased the blockade by attacking the convoy along the Mekong River that brought all the military supplies and food to the capital.

I understood at that time that it had come to the point when we had two options left. The first option consisted of using the international airport as a supply line. I think the American advisor rejected this because it was too costly to operate, and the war might have been prolonged. The Americans already had a secret plan to cut all aid to South Vietnam and Cambodia before walking away. The second option consisted of trying to reoccupy some strategic positions along the Mekong River that had fallen into the hands of the communists at the beginning of the war. The CIA and the American advisor accepted this one. However, it was a death sentence to all the soldiers in the Cambodian army who carried out that mission. As a young lieutenant and pilot, my heart dropped from the time the plan was on the drawing board. I did not know who pushed the envelope this far, the American advisor, Lon Nol's chief of staff, or both. Until now, nobody asked, talked about, or took full responsibility about this failed mission. This is the first time in forty years that I brought it to life.

Here is my criticism.

At that time, the Cambodian armed forces were fighting a desperate war, and for defensive purposes only. This operation was very costly to human life, especially to our remaining elite troops. We sent them to die and let the communists slaughter them like animals without having a chance to say good-bye to their loved ones. More importantly, they lost in battle. The reason I bring this subject to you is that with a big operation like this, the American advisor could have stopped or taken action, because the Americans controlled all the hardware, food, and weaponry, while the Cambodians provided only the manpower.

It is possible that the American advisor wanted to close this chapter of war a little bit early.

To understand this part of failure, please go back to the beginning of the war with me when Lon Nol and Sirik Matak were backed by the CIA and toppled Prince Sihanouk. The Vietcong invaded Cambodia immediately. The strategic positions along the Mekong River were taken over and remained under their control from the beginning despite Cambodia having great support from sophisticated fighters, bombers, and 24-hour protection from the US Air Force and the South Vietnamese navy gunboats. The Cambodian army still could not hold on to the positions with their conventional weapons.

Four and a half years later, we sent our elite troops on a one-way ticket with only their weaponry. They were shipped by navy boats to the position, and given less than five minutes to get out, climb the river bank, and take over to defend the position. But this time they didn't have support from the US Air Force and South Vietnamese navy. By the time the army took and defended the position, less than 24 hours later they were surrounded by the communists who bled them to death one by one.

The Cambodian air force at that time used less than 50% of it normal forces because of the lack of spare parts. The stupid part of this mission was that there were no plans to evacuate the injured, to resupply, or to reinforce at all. The resupply line at that time involved dropping supplies from a helicopter at 3000 feet onto a field smaller than a football field. These new strategies did not slow down the communists from attacking the convoy. The American advisor knew exactly when the dry season was coming, but we were not able to use the Mekong as a supply line anyway because the river gets smaller and shallower while the riverbank gets steeper. This was a favorable time for the communists to attack. Why did they still launch this stupid operation?

I did not know exactly how many battalions were slaughtered by the communist at that time. And now the Chinese and Russians provided the communists, for the first time, with state-of-the-art underwater mines to end the flow of traffic along the Mekong River. Now the mission was useless, and the soldiers that were trapped along the Mekong River were fighting for their lives. There was no way to retrieve them. I saw the flaw from the beginning, but I had no power to stop and save the lives of our elite troops who we could have used later to protect the capital. This kind of operation should not have been on the drawing board. As forward air control pilot, I can't erase from my memory some of the final messages from our brave soldiers that were sent to their loved ones through my friends and me before they committed suicide rather than be captured and tortured by the communists. They were also running out of bullets and food.

One morning when I arrived at Pochentong Air Base in the capital, two strange-looking bombs were hanging under the wings of a T-28 parked inside the protected bunker. It was longer, bigger, and heavier than the MK 82 (500 lbs.) bomb, and it looked cigar like. My squadron leader, Maj. Ly Sophean, told us in secret that they were nerve gas bombs. The only person who was allowed to carry out the mission was Lt. Col. Pheav Kim Seang. He survived the war, escaped to Thailand alone without his family, and then decided to repatriate back to Cambodia where he was slaughtered by the Khmer Rouge. We used that type of bomb twice a week to stop and slow down the aggressive movement of the communists toward the capital, and for the protection of troops along the Mekong River and around the vital Pochentong air base under the code name CBU-55.

I was told one of the missions was not successful when the wind shifted direction. One of the army's positions that was surrounded by the Khmer Rouge

Unfortunate Cambodia

and Vietcong along the Mekong River was covered by a cloud produced by the bombs and we did not hear any radio calls again. It was very sad as a human being and a pilot myself, but I prefer our heroes killed that way rather than tortured to death.

Chapter 8
Trusting the Americans Until the End

When John Gunther Dean became ambassador to Cambodia, I knew something big might happen. I remembered during the 1960s when he had been ambassador to South Vietnam. There were military coups almost every month until Ngo Did Diem died in a coup d'état. The American advisor or the State Department at that time should have given the Cambodian people an ultimatum: fight until the last drop of their blood, surrender to the United Nations, or drop their weapons and run. There would have been no more military aid in the future and this might have saved a lot of lives. The Cambodian people still trusted the Americans until the last minute when the Americans pulled out of the capital. They did not see behind the smiling face of Ambassador Dean.

Unfortunate Cambodia

All the Cambodian planes in the background retagged as American, 1975.

When I arrived at camp San Onofre as a refugee, I worked as a volunteer and met the Marine captain who was in charge. He told me that the portion of the camp that accommodated the Cambodian refugees at that time was supposed to be demolished, but one month before the fall of the Cambodian government, his superior gave the order to fix it instead to accommodate the refugees. For me, it was so clear that the State Department was already preparing the Cambodian funeral while they were still alive and fighting. The Cambodians themselves in Cambodia still believed the Americans never left them.

When the Americans pulled out on April 12, 1975, the State Department expected the Cambodian armed forces to lay down their arms on the same day.

Despite that we were running out of fuel and bullets, we still fought with whatever we had left because we knew the consequences of this conflict better than the Americans did. Finally, the American Congress felt ashamed and decided to give $52 million in military aid to Cambodia. The money, equipment, fuel, bullets, and food did not arrive in time.

The war game was over. At that time, I was in Udorn, Thailand, with a US military assistant. One of the US personnel told us that they still had radio contact with one of the female radio operators in Kg. Spoeu Province, Cambodia, until the last second. Her words were, "The Khmer Rouge [is] at the front gate. What do you want me to do?"

The Americans in Bangkok did not answer.

And her last words were, "Now he is standing in front of my desk."

The mysterious lady and her voice became silenced forever.

During the war, the CIA brought the Cambodian-born Vietnamese soldiers trained by the Green Berets named Mike's Force into Cambodia to help fight the Vietcong and the Khmer Rouge from South Vietnam. They were the great fighters, but unfortunately they paid the higher price at the end of the war because when they came to Cambodia, they brought with them their entire families. The worst part of it all was when they spoke. They still had an accent that the Khmer Rouge could easily identify, and the Khmer Rouge despised them the most. At the same time when the war ended, they were trapped inside Cambodia with no way to get back to their native country of Vietnam, which was part of Cambodia over 100 years ago. Most of them were then slaughtered by the Khmer Rouge.

I had a reliable source tell me after the war had ended and President Ford had ordered all the Americans out of Cambodia that during the evacuation out of Phnom Penh on April 12, 1975, some of the Cambodian generals had suggested to the Cambodian army chief of staff to use the tanks to block their exit, take all the Americans hostage for military aid ransom, and punish them for their involvement. Most of them turned down the suggestion. They preferred to let all the Americans and Ambassador Dean go free, and they stayed behind to let the communists slaughter them and their entire families. We were betrayed by the Americans. All our great generals at that time were Buddhists, which is why we chose not to avenge but rather swallow the pain that was created by the Americans.

I was in shock when I heard that the State Department did not give seats to freedom-seeking

Cambodians during the evacuation, not even to our very best generals that helped the Americans fight the communists until the end, with the exception of Lon Nol's right hand man, Gen. Sirik Matak. He was the one who collaborated with the CIA from the beginning to bring down the king. However, Gen. Sirik Matak replied by thanking Ambassador Dean for the offer and handing him a letter in his handwriting that produced a mixture of sorrow and foreboding in Washington. He preferred to stay behind.

In the letter he said:

"I cannot, alas, leave in such a cowardly fashion." And later in the same letter he added, "If I shall die here on the spot and in my country that I love, it is too bad, but we were all born and must die one day. I have only committed this mistake of believing in you 'the Americans.'"

In the letter, he did not mention any names at all, but he admitted he made the greatest mistake in his life by collaborating with the Americans to bring down the king and lead his six million Cambodians to help the Americans fight the communist Vietcong. In the end, the Americans abandoned the Cambodians with no regrets whatsoever.

During the war, my best friend Lt. Pech Lim Kuon and I both loved the American people since

Unfortunate Cambodia

we were very young, but we both hated American policy and the way they started the Cambodian war. We had no choice but to join the Americans in fighting the Khmer Rouge and the Vietcong. Lt. Pech Lim Kuon was the one who dropped the bombs on the Cambodian presidential conference building at Chamkar Morn, Phnom Penh, in 1973. Lon Nol escaped unharmed. In his first dive, he had already hit his target. He still had 2 MK 82 bombs. The American embassy was located less than a mile away. Imagine if he had hated the Americans, he could have wiped out the American embassy and all their personnel during his second dive, but instead he preferred to hit the same target. He was successful, escaped, and landed his T-28 in the province of Kratié, where he was put under house arrest by the Khmer Rouge until the end of the war. The Khmer Rouge knew he did not like them, but the Khmer Rouge made a big mistake by forgetting to kill him right away. Later, when the war ended, he had the genius plan to trick the Chinese instructor and advisor by taking off in one of the Khmer Rouge's helicopters (UH-1 Iroquois) and made a great escape into Thailand. The French government pulled him out of Thailand immediately for political and safety reasons before the Thai government could sell him back to the Khmer Rouge. Now he lives in

Paris under the assumed named Pascal Lim. We are both still great, trusted friends.

The war ended on April 17, 1975, at 0800 and at 0900 Col. Norodom Vatvani, the person in charge of all Cambodian personnel in Udorn, Thailand, received a phone call from the US High Command in Bangkok. He asked that the Cambodian pilots and volunteers fly back to Cambodia with the American pilot and airplane that was used to carry fuel, the personnel for reason to evacuate the entire families because there were a lot of airplanes left behind, but there was no fuel and pilots to fly out. They told us it was very simple; they did the stop and go landing and dropped all of us off with the fuel. The rest was up to us, to refuel the plane and take off.

I was in shock to hear of this stupid operation, but this time they asked for volunteers. I was the only one who stood up to asked a few questions about safety on the ground, who was controlling the airfield, and how the operation was planned. Two hours later they scrapped the mission. In less than 24 hours, all the Cambodian airplanes on the tarmac at that American air base were retagged as American planes. If this kind of operation would have launched, none of us would have gotten out alive. I was finally able to fully understand, for the last time, that this was an

Unfortunate Cambodia

underhanded scheme to use the surviving Cambodian pilots, including me, to retrieve the hardware that was left behind for them.

Thank you, CHRIST, you saved my life, and I am able to tell my painful story to the world.

Chapter 9
**Why Did It Take So Long for
the Vietnamese to Rescue Cambodia?**

Look back at the past 600-year history between the Cambodians and the Vietnamese. In regard to war, the invasions never stopped until early 1863 when the French took over Laos, Vietnam, and Cambodia. At that time, the Vietnamese had already taken a big portion of Cambodian territory, and Cambodia was nearly wiped out. The French redrew the boundaries for each country, gave them sovereignty, and created constitutions. Each country was ruled by a king, but they remained French protectorates. In addition, the French reclaimed Battambang and Siem Reap from Thailand, but it was too late for one country, formerly named Champa, located on the eastern side of Cambodia. That entire country, culture, and language was swallowed up and wiped out by the overpopulated Vietnam.

After the Khmer Rouge took over Lon Nol's regime in 1975, they separated the Cambodian-born

Vietnamese from the rest of the population. They did not kill or torture this group of people, but they returned all of them to Vietnam. In addition, the Khmer Rouge kicked out the Vietcong, who had helped them win the war in Cambodia. That sparked anger from the communist Vietcong, but they kept quiet. And then the Khmer Rouge started committing violent acts against its own people, which the world had never heard of, by torturing, starving, killing, and burying them alive. They preferred to use knives, shovels, axes, ropes, and plastic bags for suffocating their victims instead of bullets. They did not believe in brainwashing or rehabilitation, only killing. Believe it or not, all these acts were carried out under Chinese supervision with thousands of agents all over Cambodia.

The communist Vietnamese knew for hundreds of years that the Cambodian people never trusted or liked them because they were the ones who had stolen their land and killed their predecessors nonstop, but this time the communist Vietnamese were patient and used different techniques to sway the Cambodian heart. They knew of the killings in Cambodia, but they did not make their move right away. They learned from previous experiences and mistakes, and waited for the right moment to come.

The right moment was during the four and a half years that Cambodia suffered the atrocities of the Khmer Rouge, when two million lives were lost and many others suffered. There was no help and no hope from any direction, even from any god on the planet. At last, the communist Vietcong moved in to kick the Khmer Rouge out. Before the invasion, did the communist Vietcong send a letter or make a phone call to the United Nations or any international press to inform them of the purpose of this invasion? The answer is no. It was so clear that this was not an act of liberation.

The Vietcong were successful for the second time, but this was different from the 1940 and 1970 invasions because the surviving Cambodians were split among their country. Half loved and thanked the communist Vietcong, who were seen as gods for saving their lives, and the other half still understood, remembered, and considered them as killers, hypocrites, and creators of all kinds of pain and suffering. They were the ones who created the Khmer Rouge and fought side by side with them. During this invasion, they brought with them approximately one million extremely impoverished Vietnamese to settle down in Cambodia and create more social problems than already existed. During their ten years of occupation, they secretly eliminated all the patriotic Cambodians for opening the door to the new era of Cambodia, and rewrote history the way they wanted to.

Now for the first time, the whole world started to wake up by boycotting the Vietnamese economy. After ten years of occupation, the economy in Vietnam had deteriorated. They knew that they could not hold on to Cambodia any longer. They needed help from outside world. They finally let the Cambodians go free, but the country was still under their cloud.

Chapter 10
To the United Nations and International Press

After Lon Nol's regime, which was backed by the CIA, unconstitutionally brought down King Sihanouk, the Red Army blood-thirsty Vietcong invaded Cambodia and took control of 75% of the country, crippling the economy and cutting off almost all communication in less than sixty days. They killed any of our people who refused to cooperate with them.

The international press was stationed in Cambodia and the UN refused to tell the world the truth behind this invasion. They preferred to lie. I still remember during the first six months of fighting along Highway No. 4, which linked the main seaport Sihanouk Ville to the capital, the Vietcong captured and held seven western reporters from the international press, including one woman, Ms. K. Webb and later released them all. I assumed they met their captors, the Vietcong. All Cambodians at the time were waiting for the truth of this incident to be released. Instead, they never mentioned their captors or the Vietcong to the world.

Later, during the raid on the capital, the Vietcong blew up the fuel storage at Prek Phnoeuv. They destroyed planes on the ground at the military airbase at Pochentong. The Vietcong personnel who carried out that suicide mission did not intend to just destroy, kill, or die. If all of you, my readers, looked closely with me to examine this incident, you would see that they were very cruel, calculated murderers. They wore no shoes, some of them no shirts, and only shorts. They carried as many plastic explosives on their bodies as they could. You know why? Because they knew their mission was to destroy and kill as many people as they could, and die, and they preferred to leave the shirts and shoes behind for their fighting Vietcong comrades. Shoes and shirts for them were the most valuable items during that war. The Cambodian armed forces were still not well equipped, and the Khmer Rouge army did not exist yet. They surprised us at that time, but our elite heroes, Mike's Force and the Cambodian-born-Vietnamese, were able to kill dozens of them while the rest escaped into the woods.

When the sun rose, the cleanup began. Cambodia was a poor country, and we did not have the proper equipment or specially trained personnel to handle dead bodies. We used trucks to haul the dead Vietcong by throwing them into them. Alas, the international press came and took pictures and videos to criticize and label the Cambodian's handling of the invaders' dead bodies as inhuman. They destroyed Cambodian pride and dignity, and showed favor toward the killing machine, the invading Vietcong. None of the international press used the word "Vietcong" or identified them as the raiders of the capital despite the dead bodies looking different from Cambodians, and the Khmer Rouge did not exist yet.

On behalf of all of the surviving and suffering Cambodian born people, our blood is still boiling toward the actions of the United Nations and the international press during that time. Both of them lied to their members, readers, and the world regarding the real invasion from the red army blood-thirsty Vietcong. I still do not understand why they have never mentioned to the world the words, "Vietcong invaded Cambodia," until now. Maybe the color of our skin or our Buddhist religion played a big role in this conflict, or perhaps we are the real unfortunate people, the descendants of the Khmer empire who built Angkor Wat that was carved in stone with the

Unfortunate Cambodia

Khmer language, just to be hated by the modern society of the twentieth century.

I write every word of this book with Cambodian blood, tears, pain, and suffering that I held in my chest for 37 years for peace, not to avenge, persecute, or hate anyone.

Before the coup, the Khmer Rouge did not have an army yet, only their high-ranking members—Kiev Sam Phan, Hou Nim, Hou Yun, Ierng Sary, Pol Pot, Chuon Mom, Chuon Choeurn, Nuon Chea, and Nong Suon—but all were held under house arrest by the king's secret police. The rest could not make any moves because they had few guns and no support from any other country. The China, Russia, and the Eastern bloc countries were friendly to the king. The king himself did not like the communists, but his brilliant techniques kept the blood-thirsty Vietcong away for a decade. Remember the King that kicked the Vietminh out of Cambodia in 1953. The extremely impoverished Cambodians were still behind the king.

Both the UN and International press still owed my people an apology. In my opinion, both of them at that time were hiding the truth from the world. You were the eyes and ears of the world for peace, but you played politics instead, and left six millions Cambodian, two and a half million dead, to suffer. My suffering, the surviving Cambodians, and the dead are still waiting for your words 42 years later.

At that time the UN was heavily influenced by three countries—the United States, China, and the Soviet Union—and they were the ones who got involved in the Cambodian conflict. That is why all of you preferred to close your eyes and ears for the blood-thirsty communist Vietcong to take over my peaceful land in less than sixty days without saying a word. On the European side, they sympathized with the communists. ONLY CHRIST KNEW.

Here is an insight—one gunman walks toward a crowd of people aiming his gun at the face of one victim, pulling the trigger, and putting his gun down in front of that group of people. When the police arrest that person and take him to court, most likely that killer would be convicted. But this case is not closed yet, right?

I am not a criminal prosecutor, but in the Cambodians' case, all of you closed the case. We have to consider:

What was the motive?
Who provided the murder weapon?
Was it a hire?
Was it a conspiracy?
Who was behind the killer?

Unfortunate Cambodia

Who helped finance the murder?

Now look back at the atrocities in Cambodia committed by the Khmer Rouge. I agree in this case that the Khmer Rouge killed at least two million lives, but I'm surprised that all the smartest and highly-educated people on earth, the members of the UN and international press, closed the Cambodians' case by closing their eyes and ears and pointing their fingers at the Khmer Rouge alone. I am now on a lonely crusade, and with CHRIST over my head, I hope to open this case to the world. In addition, the whole world chose to reward Dr. Kissinger and Le Doc Tho with the Nobel Peace Prize. For me, one of them doused the gasoline on Cambodia while the other one lit the match.

After Cambodia became independent in 1953, and up until the coup in 1970, Cambodia was an oasis of peace. When the Vietnam War escalated, the United States tried to persuade Cambodia to help fight, but they were turned down by the brilliant King Sihanouk. He preferred to be a speaker for the communists, and he condemned all the American actions toward the Vietcong in order to extract peace from them. That sparked the anger and frustration of the Americans toward the king.

It took the Americans over a decade to overthrow the king, which I previously mentioned in chapter 4. It took over a decade for the mouth-watering, blood-thirsty Vietcong to find an excuse to invade the peaceful land of Cambodia and colonize it at the same time. All these actions were fully funded by the Chinese and Russians, and they were the ones who created and armed the Khmer Rouge. During the killing under the Khmer Rouge, the Chinese advisors were all over Cambodia. They taught the Khmer Rouge to fly the helicopters that were left behind by the Cambodian Air Force. This story was told by my trusted friend Pascal Lim. He was the one who dropped the bombs at the presidential palace that I mentioned in chapter 8. The Chinese knew exactly what the Khmer Rouge did to their people, and they had the power to stop or change the course any time they wanted to, but they preferred to ignore it instead.

The Khmer rouge was a very small satellite of the Chinese. If the Khmer Rouge leader disobeyed any Chinese rule or did anything the Chinese did not like, that Khmer Rouge leader or person would be replaced or killed in less than forty-eight hours. If we look back at the Korean War, the communist Chinese sent a quarter million Chinese soldiers on a one way ticket to die on the Korean peninsula simply to show the world how brutal they were.

During the 1979 invasion by the Vietcong, because of the fast approach of the Vietcong, the Chinese advisor and the high-ranking Khmer Rouge did not have enough time to escape. The Beijing government paid the Thai government to evacuate them by helicopter from inside Cambodia to Thailand and China. If you look closely at the evidence that I have stated in all the chapters, the Vietcong, Americans, Chinese, and Russians were LIABLE for the deaths of more than two million lives, in addition to the pain, suffering, and billions of dollars in property damage in the Cambodian conflict.

After the World War II ended, and up until 1979, the Vietminh, a predecessor of the Vietcong, and the Vietcong, both invaded, infiltrated, and occupied Cambodia three times. They killed at least half a million Cambodians while torturing many others. The United Nations knew this but preferred to remain silent. They did not see the way I saw it, because the Vietcong was the right hand man of the Russians and the Chinese, and the Vietcong played a big role in spreading communism. The Chinese and Russians had great influence with the United Nations.

If we look back over 600 years, not a single Cambodian went in Vietnam or Thailand to steal territory from them. They were the ones who killed us and stole our land nonstop. I feel sad for my unfortunate people. We have been natives of this land since the first century "FUNAN." We are descendants of the people who built Angkor Wat. During our dark ages, 1432-1863, we lost the Mekong Delta to Vietnam and more land to the Thai. Our race and culture had been nearly wiped out by the Thai and Vietnamese, but thanks to the French who came to rescue us, and of course our great friends the Americans who helped Lon Nol's government fight the communists.

More than half a million tons in bombs, equal to three and a half times the bombs dropped on Japan, were dropped on Cambodia by the US Air Force, killing at least 100,000 innocent lives, and causing billions of dollars in structural damage. During the twentieth century when the Vietnam War had almost ended, the superpowers used us as a steppingstone, and their ACTIONS sent us nearly back to the Stone Age, yet all of you, until now, still pretend that you did not see it the way that I saw it.

Despite that, I still practice Buddhism, and my heart changes little by little. Only Christ could understand this as being one of the biggest world conspiracies of the twentieth century. I am not alone, that is why the Romans converted to Christianity 1,500 years ago. I hope my people will one day act in the same way as the Romans did. In the United States alone, about 35% of Cambodians have converted to Christianity and a lot more will be on the way. May Christ bless and protect my unfortunate people and country. THANK YOU, LORD.

Chapter 11
To the American People

First off, I must say that I am proud to be an American. We are a unique nation, far different from the rest of the world. In my preface, I begged my readers not to view this book as criticism or hatred toward my beloved and adopted country, the United States of America. All citizens of the United States are very kind toward any race or religion. They are innocent people. They obey the law, and are not afraid to criticize their politicians or leaders for what they believe. They open their doors to any race or religion with no discrimination at all. They are not afraid or too proud to sacrifice their loved ones for someone else's interests, or for freedom around the world. I am not afraid to commend the good deeds that the United States has carried out for the rest of the world. On behalf of Cambodians, we thank you very much for all you have done to help us, including those who have settled down in the United States and those at home in Cambodia right now.

Unfortunate Cambodia

After the Khmer Rouge took control of Cambodia in 1975, I was still a refugee in Thailand. The war had already ended, but there was still an incident between the United States and the Khmer Rouge government. I did not understand why the CIA toyed with the Khmer Rouge government by sending a merchant ship, the *Mayaguez*, equipped with sophisticated electronics, back and forth in international waters or in Cambodian waters in hopes of provoking them. The Khmer Rouge gunboat seized that merchant ship. The war had already ended and the Americans let the Khmer Rouge win that war.

I am not criticizing the actions of the Americans, but I feel sorry for the loss of more than forty young heroic and brave Marines. In my opinion, it could have been avoided. The crew of the ship was made up of mostly foreigners. Why did President Ford give the green light to launch the risky operation of rescuing the crew? From what I heard from a radio broadcast of the Khmer Rouge at the time, they did not want to challenge the Americans at all. The Americans, at that time, overreacted and still had a lot of options on the table.

The reason I bring this story to you, my fellow Americans, is because of my sorrow for the loss of these young Marines and all other American lives that helped Cambodian forces fight the communists in Cambodia. They are still in my heart.

Please accept my condolences to you, Americans, and especially the families who sacrificed their loved ones in this Cambodian conflict. The Cambodian people and all you Americans were victims of this conflict created by the wrong policies of President Nixon, Dr. Kissinger, and their advisors.

During the war, the Americans dropped more than half a million tons of bombs on Cambodia, which was equal to 3½ times those used in Japan, killing at least 100,000 innocent lives. In addition, there were billions of dollars in damages to the structures by these attacks. So far, Americans have slowly helped to rebuild or construct new buildings, schools, and hospitals in Cambodia. Thankfully, the US government sent the garment industry to Cambodia through Chinese entrepreneurs, but most of the money goes into the pockets of these Chinese who exploit young Cambodian workers. I hope one day, with all your voices, we can improve and change this problem. Americans have the power to turn the clock back. Please help us restore democracy and human rights, and please send better paying jobs to these people. America made Thailand a super rich country in the region, and sent a lot of high paying jobs to the Cambodian butchers—the ex-Vietcong. Why not throw a bone to the one who was caught in the middle of this conflict. Now America becomes Vietnam's godfather because of the South China Sea conflict.

Lastly, with Christ's help, I still have a dream that America will one day tell the current Vietnamese government to stop abusing Cambodia (enough is enough). On behalf of Cambodian garment factory workers and me, we thank you America—you put food on the plates of very poor Cambodians, and made their lives a little better. I can't imagine Cambodia without these 400,000 jobs.

May CHRIST bless my adopted country, the United States of America.

Thank you, United States.

Chapter 12
To My Fellow Cambodians

My fellow Cambodians, I apologize if I went too far right or too far left in my opinions. I actually do not belong to any clans or political party at all. My purpose in writing this book is to release our pain and suffering, which I have kept in my chest for forty years. The whole world ignored the greatest conspiracy and its consequences by pointing a finger at the Khmer Rouge alone. I know that some parts of my book will be disagreeable and disliked by many of you, but this is my book, my opinions, my expressions, my freedom of speech, and I take full responsibility for the content of it. I wrote this book for peaceful purposes, and not to convey hate or avenge any neighboring countries or persons.

On our behalf, my countrymen, it is important to remember, and not to forget, all the killings, stealing of our land, raping, and torturing of our ancestors that have occurred over the past 600 years and still continues. Our neighboring countries only wait for the right opportunity to destroy, weaken, and make us fight each other, causing us to have a miserable life or to disappear from our land. Right now, our population is approximately eleven million, but we are sandwiched by the Thai and Vietnamese. Each of them has a population nearing eighty million. Please be aware of it and alert. What will happen to us in the next 100 years? Who will protect us? Anybody?

I have in-depth vision and only one solution in mind that will most likely help save and restore our land and culture during the next century, but I need your cooperation. I will tell you at the end of this chapter.

During our dark ages, 1432-1863, we lost the Mekong Delta to Vietnam and a lot more land to the Thai, but the story did not end there. Remember, my countrymen, when the French arrived in 1863, our population was only a few hundred thousand, mostly elders and the sick. We were nearly wiped out by two killers: the Vietnamese and Thai. They kept slaughtering us nonstop. They did not just want our land, they wanted us to be wiped off the map to take over our land and rewrite history.

Remember, we are the descendants of the Khmer who built Angkor Wat. We had our language and inscriptions carved in stone for thousands of years thanks to our great heroes and great ancestors, who spilled their blood to protect our land. It is with great thanks to them that we still exist, are able to still speak the same language, and are still able to be called Khmer.

I clearly understood the 1979 invasion of the communist Vietnamese to kick the Khmer Rouge out. Some of you thank and consider them as gods for doing so, but do not forget what they have done to us for 600 years. Now I invite all of you take a deep breath with me and look back and ask ourselves some questions.

Did the Communist Vietnamese tell the United Nations or international press the purpose of the 1979 invasion before they moved in?

The answer is "NO."

Did they inform the United Nations that this invasion was to save Cambodian lives from the jaws of the Khmer Rouge?

The answer is "NO."

All of this was nothing more than hypocritical actions that their ancestors did to our people over the past 600 years.

During my lifetime, until 1979, the communist Vietnamese invaded our land three times with the intention of stealing land and killing at least half a million of our innocent people, not including those subjected to torture. I have a great story to tell you today, my countrymen. The Vietcong do not want the future generations of Cambodians to know or to remember at all.

Battle of SRE CHEH in 1953

After Cambodia became independent in 1953, the Vietminh, a predecessor of the Vietcong, refused to leave our land. In addition, they tried to grab hold of Cambodia's two northeastern provinces, Kratié and Stoeung Treng. At that time, our great young king, Norodom Sihanouk, sent our best heroes, the airborne division, with the conventional weapons that were left behind by the French to face the blood-thirsty war machine. Our heroes at that time promised all Cambodians that they would fight until the last drop of their blood was shed. We used city buses to transport them to the battlefield with a one-way ticket to hold and protect these two provinces. With brilliant plans and their bravery, they defeated the Vietminh in this battle despite the fact that they outnumbered us. In the end, the multilateral peace accord ordered all of them out of Cambodia anyway. You can now imagine how much anger was building inside the communist Vietnamese system.

My fellow Cambodians, I do not mind what side you choose to stand behind, but this is a painful memory for me and for all our future generations. When you travel from downtown Siem Reap toward Angkor Wat, there is a high school named Lycee Suryavarman II on your right-hand side. After the 1970 coup, during which time the Khmer Rouge was not in existence, the Red Army Vietcong surrounded and tried to take over that school. From the beginning, Lon Nol's government used volunteer high school students and teachers armed with World War II weapons, to protect the school. Surprisingly, the students and teachers with their bravery were able to hold their position for seven days until the army moved up to liberate them. I do not know how many lives were lost during that assault. I wrote this small paragraph for the memory of one young brave teenage girl named Deap Vanara, and to everyone that helped in protecting the school. Deap Vanara was shot and killed by a Vietcong sniper, who was using a state-of-the-art long-range rifle provided by the Russians, when she refused to give up her school to the Vietcong invaders. One of the survivors of that assault, a teacher named Tan Than, now resides in Paris, France, but he paid a high price having lost his eyesight to a Vietcong's hand grenade. Always remember, during the past 600 years when the Vietnamese captured and killed our best heroes, the ones who fought to protect and save this land for our future generations. Some of them were not killed right away. They were burned alive, such as DAM TE ONG.

In 1962, the International Court in The Hague ordered the Thai government to surrender Prasat Preah Vihear back to Cambodia. Less than one month later, the Thai army took it back by force. Prince Sihanouk at that time used different tactics by sending his two brave commanders, Maj. Tiep Ben and Maj. Ky Hack, in along with their men. For two weeks, they secretly went through the jungle and climbed steep slopes to reach the top of the Dangrek mountain range, and with a bloody assault, Cambodians reclaimed the territory. When the news broke, I was in shock, and so happy and proud of our great heroes who carried out that impossible mission, because we were like tiny mice who were forced to go up against a great elephant in battle. But the Thai did not give up. They later launched many bloody assaults in an attempt to regain the land, but they failed. Perhaps due to the pressure from international observers, the Thai never tried to take the land back again by force.

I know some of you wanted to build a big monument in thanks to the Vietnamese invasions that helped kick-out the Khmer Rouge, saving many Cambodian lives. I have no objection to this idea, but in my opinion, if you choose to build one, make sure you build two monuments—one to show your gratitude, and the other for the torture, massacres, stealing of land, pain, and suffering that our people were subjected to continuously for the past 600 years. Remember, they were the ones who created the Khmer Rouge and fought side by side with them. From the end of World War II up until 1979, they killed at least half a million Cambodians, not including those subjected to pain, torture, and suffering.

Remember, my countrymen, after World War II alone, the Chinese had helped the Vietnamese communists win two wars, one against the French and another one with the Americans. Now, would you please take a deep breath with me and look inside their hypocritical minds? If the Chinese made the Vietnamese pay all this debt, it might have taken them more than a thousand years to do so, but instead they kicked the Chinese out and shot them with their own guns. With this kind of attitude and behavior over the past 600 years toward our people, what do you still think of them?

I know some of you have become extremely wealthy, and I beg all of you to look after our poor and needy. When we will leave this world, we'll leave empty-handed anyway, and I beg you all to stop fighting each other for power or money. It is time for us to join hands to work together and correct the mistakes, and change the course and lead our country to success and peace. With your cooperation, we can help heal the wounds and eliminate some scars that were left behind by the war, and remember the war itself did not belong to us. I wrote this book for peaceful purposes only. If my book becomes a success, my name will be well known to you all. I will dedicate the rest of my life to all of your interests only. I knew my hands had Cambodian blood on them, too, as you already know, but would you please forgive me? At that time, I only had two choices, which I mentioned in chapter 4.

You already know that the countries that had Cambodian blood on their hands walked away free. Worst of all, right now, the same ones keep doing the same things over and over because the surviving Cambodians did not use the right medicine to cure this disease. My strategy is telling the world the truth and bringing them to justice. Look at how they pretend that they did not know, hear, or see anything. During the Vietnam War, the Americans were using Cambodia to fight the communist Vietcong. And the cost was two million lives, and two million landmines planted in Cambodia that killed, crippled, and caused blindness.

All of them were made in China. Please do not forget the Chinese were the ones who fully funded and equipped the Vietcong with sophisticated weapons to invade our land, kill our people, and create the Khmer Rouge. Right now, the Americans and the rest of the world are closing their eyes and ears again and allowing the current Vietnamese government (ex-Vietcong) to colonize Laos & Cambodia. Class action lawsuits might work, or at list prove to the world that they can no longer hide their hypocritical minds and abuse Cambodians from Vietnam.

Have you noticed the behavior of the tribunal court for the Khmer Rouge run by the international teams? They put three top Khmer Rouge leaders on trial and they never indicted anybody but these three.

OH, Lord, for me this is the greatest conspiracy of the twentieth century and the modern civilized world of the superpowers. If you are dig deeper into their closet with me, all of the international judges and their staff who work this case became fat cats by sucking the sweat, blood, and tears of the suffering Cambodians. Hundreds of million of dollars went into the pockets of the people who ran the court.

The suffering of the Cambodian nation and their people benefited nothing from this court. There is nothing to prevent a future Cambodian holocaust from repeating, or stopping the abuse from neighboring Cambodia.

Once again my fellow Cambodians, our land is shrinking. To protect our priceless real estate, Cambodian culture, and sovereignty, we should convert our religion from Buddhism to Christianity. Please forgive me if my idea is too radical for you. I still practice Buddhism. In my own opinion, this is the best option we have. Christianity, so far for me, is still the best religion on the planet. They are the ones who reach out, help, and protect the rest of the world with no discrimination whatsoever, and we all need this kind of help. We have practiced Buddhism for the past 800 years, and we are dwindling. We need to practice something with which we can survive. I can be wrong, but I could never go wrong with CHRISTIANITY.

I thank you all very much, and please forgive me. May Christ and Buddha bless and protect our sovereignty and our people for the next century and beyond.

I thank you all with my great respect, trust, deep smile, and love.

Chapter 13
The Big Mistake of the King

I still consider and agree that King Norodom Sihanouk was a great politician during this time. During his reign, Cambodian had only 20,000 armed men, which included the police forces. He led his country toward peace, and provided his six million people with harmony, happiness, and prosperity. Even though Cambodia was a poor country, he was still able to provide his people with free education and healthcare.

Corruption existed, but on a very small scale. He was the one who balanced the peace within the region. Imagine, he was able to protect Cambodian sovereignty and peace without firing a shot or losing land, and Cambodia remained untouchable to the communist Vietcong for over a decade.

Remember, he was the one who reclaimed Prasat Preah Vihear from the Thai in 1962, and he was the one who kicked all the Vietminh out of Cambodia in 1953.

Unfortunate Cambodia

After the unconstitutional coup that was backed by the CIA removed him from power, he was upset, angry, frustrated, and depressed. In my opinion, he made one mistake, and that mistake alone almost wiped out every good thing that he had done for his people and his country in the past.

That mistake was to order all his followers to leave town and join the Vietcong to fight Lon Nol, who was backed by the US government. However, most Cambodians did not follow his request because everybody hated and never trusted the Vietcong. After the suffering, the pain, and the loss of more than two million lives, some of his followers tried to blame him.

In my opinion, if the King had retired from politics and kept quiet for a while, and then returned to politics, the entire Cambodian population would have still considered him a god-like king. Instead, he went to China and became a speaker against his own people that had fought the Vietcong invaders. But despite everything, I still respect and salute him as a great, great Cambodian icon and a great, great hero at that time. The CIA and Dr. Kissinger destroyed him and his reputation.

Dr. Kissinger, President Nixon, the CIA, and all the advisors hated him, his politics, and the way he protected his people at that time. They were the ones who turned Cambodia upside down.

Chapter 14
To My Neighboring Thailand and Vietnam

Once again, I write this book for peaceful purposes only. We have never stopped fighting or killing one another, but for the past 600 years most of the fighting, killing, and invasions were sparked by either the Thai or Vietnamese. Whatever you both attained from us, keep it, but I beg you both not to take or kill anymore.

Our main religion is Buddhism, but it was a shame. During the communist Vietnamese invasion in 1979, Cambodian civilians, women, children, orphans, and survivors of the Khmer Rouge executions and starvations needed your temporary help crossing the border into your country THAILAND. You, the Thai, welcomed them with machine guns, cannons, and rape. On the Vietnamese side, during my lifetime alone, you Vietminh and Vietcong invaded my land three times and killed at least half a million Cambodians, plus caused billions of dollars in property damage.

During your (Vietnam communist) occupation from 1979 to 1989, you were so brilliant using my people as human shields to chop down rare wood and mainly to clear land mines. You erased and rewrote our history. You secretly eliminated our patriotic Khmer and still got away. The worst part is that the whole world did not see it the way I saw it. Thousands of innocent lives were lost and damaged.

I respect both the Thai and Vietnamese citizens, but it has come to the point at which both of you should please leave Cambodians alone.

For the past 600 years, Buddha could not stop or slow down your aggressive actions toward Cambodians. From the twenty-first century and beyond, many of my fellow people and I beg CHRIST for protection. I hope with CHRIST'S help, your people and mine will change their negative attitudes toward each other. I hope one day we will look at each other with a smile, love, and trust.

Unfortunate Cambodia

Gentleman who encouraged me to write this book, AIRCDRE F.E.BURTT in 1972 (Point Cook).

Chapter 15
My Own Judgment

Without the involvement of the Americans, it is likely that Cambodia would never have gone to war. When the Vietnam War had almost ended, the Vietcong could not move into Cambodia because the king was still in power. He was the leader who had provided six million Cambodians with happiness and prosperity, and he was the only one who stood face to face against US policy and the Vietcong. This may be one of the greatest modern world conspiracies of the twentieth century, created by the superpowers and the blood-thirsty Vietcong by using six million Cambodians as steppingstones. After the coup of Lon Nol and Prince Sirik Matak, which was backed by the CIA, the Vietcong immediately invaded Cambodia with the help of the Russians and Chinese.

From then on, the bullets started to fly, and Cambodian blood started to flow like a river. The

Unfortunate Cambodia

Chinese and the Russians wanted to turn all of South East Asia into communist territory, taking over country after country. Without their armament and money, the Vietcong had only their teeth and fingernails to use as weapons. Most of the world saw the war in Cambodia as a civil war, but it was not if you look closely and examine all my evidence and logic regarding the situation. The Vietcong created the Khmer Rouge, and fought side by side and assisted them until the end of the war.

Here are my judgments:

1. If the CIA had not gotten involved and was not behind the coup...
   No killing field.

2. If there was no American aid after the coup...
   No killing field.

3. If the Vietcong had not invaded Cambodia...
   No killing field.

4. If there were no armaments and support from Russia and China to the Vietcong and Khmer Rouge...
   No killing field.

5. If Lon Nol and his gang had stayed behind the king...
   No killing field.

6. If the Americans had not abandoned Cambodia...
   No killing field.

At the end of the war the Vietcong got all of Vietnam. The Khmer Rouge got all of Cambodia. However, the Vietcong was very disappointed because the Khmer Rouge, who was backed by the Chinese, forced all of them out of the country. During my lifetime, this is the second time that the communist Vietcong were forced out of Cambodia.

At the end of Lon Nol's regime, two Khmer Rouges emerged: Chinese-backed and Vietnamese-backed Khmer Rouges. The Vietnamese Khmer Rouge wanted Cambodia to be part of Vietnam, and the Chinese Khmer Rouge wanted to be independent, but backed by the Chinese. Victory at that time belonged to the Chinese-backed Khmer Rouge led by Pol Pot. To avoid persecution, the high ranking Vietnamese-backed Khmer Rouge escaped to Vietnam and was later brought back by the Vietnamese to rule Cambodia since then, but with their own tight grip after they kicked out Pol Pot during their 1979 invasion.

The Khmer Rouge started to clean up their own organization by killing any individuals suspected of collaborating with the Vietcong, or any persons who had Vietnamese communist influence. In addition, they tried to create a new regime of Cambodian communists by committing atrocities against their own people that

Unfortunate Cambodia

the world never heard of. They were the sickest of sick people. They made the incredibly stupid mistake of killing, torturing, and starving their own people. They did not believe in rehabilitation or brainwashing.

Furthermore, believe it or not, the Khmer Rouge did all of this under Chinese supervision because the Chinese advisors were all over Cambodia during that time. The Chinese at that time could have changed the course of Cambodian history and the killings. They knew and witnessed the killings because they were the authority in the Khmer Rouge at that time. Even the high-ranking Khmer Rouge dressed themselves like the Chinese, but in black. If the Khmer Rouge leaders disobeyed any Chinese rule or did anything which the Chinese did not like it, that Khmer Rouge member could be replaced, arrested, or executed in less than 48 hours without a doubt.

My course supervisor SQNDR F.E. BURTT and me during basic training in 1972.

In the end, the Americans, Chinese, Russians, and Vietcong walked away free from the crime scene, but all of their hands were full of Cambodian blood. Their fingerprints were left all over the place. Surprisingly, the whole world cheered them and rewarded Dr. Kissinger and Le Duc Tho with Nobel Peace Prizes, and now the whole world, including the United Nations and the international press, still does not see any wrongdoing. From the way I saw it, they let these people go free.

OH, LORD! CHRIST PLEASE HELP

Chapter 16
To Dr. Kissinger and Other People Involved

During the 1960s, I was a young teenager and a student. Like most Cambodian children, I was having a wonderful time and focusing on education. Cambodia was not a particularly rich country, but we were self-sufficient. As a country, we remained rather neutral and did not wish to involve ourselves with conflict with other countries, but unfortunately our precious real estate, Cambodia, was sandwiched between Thailand and Vietnam. Despite the fact that Cambodia had less than 20,000 armed men, including police forces, we still remained untouchable to the Vietcong for over a decade.

Because Cambodia was led by a brilliant king, Norodom Sihanouk, with his genius international politics, we were able to keep both American and Vietcong hands off Cambodia. It took the Americans over a decade to overthrow the king, which I previously stated in chapter 4. The whole country was shocked and cried out loud, especially the individuals who had previous experience with the Vietminh. We knew the consequences would be great when we heard about the coup while the king was out of Cambodia.

I respect and salute you, Dr. Kissinger, and the all the people who got involved. I see you all as great politicians and American heroes. As a Cambodian American and a Republican, I am a tolerant man, a trait that I inherited from my parents. Most of you have Anglo ancestry. From my point of view and deep thought, your race and your religion of Christianity is far different from any race and religion on the planet. Looking back on the history of the world, if your ancestors committed any violent acts toward any other race, generations later you, as a people, would promote change, correct your actions, apologize for any wrong doings, and even sacrifice your loved one to ensure peace around the world.

I, with Christ looking down over my head, knew of the exact intentions behind your thinking at that time. If you knew that the consequence of the Cambodian conflict would cost more than two million Cambodian lives in addition to those subjected to torture and suffering, the history of your Anglo ancestry and your religion would have stopped all of you from getting involved in bringing down King Norodom Sihanouk's reign. The Vietnam

Unfortunate Cambodia

War was almost over and you had already planned negotiations with the North Vietnamese for the withdrawal of all American troops. Unfortunately, you underestimated the consequences of that conflict. That is why I personally forgive all your actions, but I will never forget the pain, suffering, and billions of dollars in property damage caused by your arsenals.

I know that during your lifetime on this planet, you will never have the heart to admit that you were in any way responsible or liable for the Cambodian killing field. I, however, have an deep vision and hope, Mr. Kissinger, that because of your ancestry and your religion, one of your great-great-grandchildren will grow up and learn of your political actions, and read my book. My dream is that one day, one of them will eventually apologize to my people on your behalf, and fortunately, I will personally accept his or her apology to my people on behalf of that person before he or she is even born.

I congratulate you on your Nobel Peace Prize, and I urge you to please not look back, because you have left behind a trail drenched in the blood of more than the two million Cambodian lives that will follow you for the rest of your life.

I apologize if I hit you too hard. When you leave this world, you will leave with your Nobel Peace

Prize. For me, when I will leave this world, I will leave empty-handed because I have left my agenda to the world, and will have released all the pain and suffering of my people to the rest of the world who will, I hope, rethink those past actions, understand the truth, and draw their own conclusions. In your mind, you know that my book will now serve as an X-ray machine for all my readers to finally see through your hidden thoughts and the CIA at that time.

Chapter 17
Special Thanks

One evening when I was already living in the United States, I was watching the news and saw a speech by Senator Ted Kennedy. I do not recall the purpose of that speech, but I remember that he said, "We cannot get rid of the Cambodia problem because it is our consequence." I did not know what you truly meant during your speech. I was in shock with mixed emotions. Mr. Senator, I have been on a lonely crusade, and I had no intention at the time of linking your speech to my book or to the Cambodian conflict at all.

To me, and what was in my mind at the time, I knew that it was CHRIST'S way of speaking out, and He chose you to carry on His word. I have memories as a young teenager witnessing many young and educated Cambodian citizens mourning the death of President KENNEDY, but I did not document it. Unfortunately at that time, one of the American newspapers was lying to the public by saying Cambodians were dancing in the streets in celebration of his death.

If my voice has a chance of being heard by you, I ask that you please accept the condolences for the death of your great brother and the greatest president of the United States from real Cambodians and the spirit of the ones who are no longer living, despite taking more than forty years to reach you. Most Cambodians loved America, even the children living in the countryside at that time, but politics played a heavy role. Your words were the greatest medicine that helped heal the wounds and eliminate some of the scars that were left behind by the war. I thank you with great respect for your words, and especially for Christ and your great ancestors who not just created you, but also instilled great tolerance in you.

During Cambodia's dark ages, 1432-1863, we were nearly wiped off the map. I, and many Cambodians who I know are behind me, wish to thank the French government. We will remember their help in protecting us as a country forever. We did not see the presence of the French as an intrusion at all, despite the fact that I lost two of my great-uncles—one died and the other one was left crippled for the rest of his life because of your brutality and torture. You, the French, and your country at that time, saved my existing Cambodia to preserve our culture, our language, and especially our Angkor Wat. Your great researchers and archeologists taught us to read the inscriptions on the wall of the Angkor Wat, knowledge that is now unfortunately lost.

Vive la France & Merci infiniment

On recent visits to my homeland, I saw many nongovernment organizations (NGO), Christian agencies, and some kindhearted individuals from around the world that came to provide assistance and relief to the needy, the poor, and the orphans in Cambodia. I thank you all very much for your contributions and hard work.

For Angelina Jolie and Brad Pitt, I ask that you please accept my thanks for your contributions, and for the help you gave my people in Cambodia for restoring what was lost from deforestation, clearing the mine fields, and creating jobs for the needy and poor. In addition, you healed the wounds and reduced the pain that was left behind by the war. I write this small paragraph to future Cambodian generations to remember, appreciate, and thank you both forever. Your wonderful names and faces will stay in our bloodstream for generations to come.

On the behalf of all Cambodians, I thank the International Court at The Hague for ordering the Thai government to return Prasat Preah Vihear to Cambodia in 1962. All Cambodians still believe that only the Western civilized world and CHRIST can help save our sovereignty in the next century to come.

Reverend Billy Graham, if my voice has a chance to be heard by you, would you please pray for my unfortunate people. I strongly believe that you have the power to communicate with CHRIST, and I thank you very much. I pray for your health and longevity.

Dear Mom and Dad, I thank you both for giving birth to me. Your generosity toward the needy Cambodian poor during your lifetimes helped save some of your children's lives during the Khmer Rouge regime. I admire and love the way you disciplined and raised me, even though I could not be the perfect son that you wanted me to be.

Even though I was very young at that time, I still remember, Mother, the way you hugged and comforted me during the unjust execution of my best friend by the Vietminh. The echo of that gunshot is still bouncing around inside my ear. I will forever remember your last words that were sent to me through your surviving daughter before you slipped into the coma and passed away during Pol Pot's regime. Both of your eyes were left wide open because your muscles were so weak from starvation. I still cannot believe your deep intuition that told you that your words would reach me, even though I was half a world away from you.

I beg both of you to forgive me for only one thing: the fact that I prefer Christianity over Buddhism. Mom and Dad, Cambodia needs to change its course to survive into the next century. This is our last hope. I hope your spirit will understand and forgive me. I will still respect and love Buddhism for the rest of my life, I promise you. I will one day meet you both when I will leave this world.

Lastly, I come to a very special gentleman who encouraged me to write this book and make it happen, AIRCDRE F.E. BURTT. Without your encouragement this story would have gone to the grave with me without a doubt. I will see you Down Under soon in some day ahead.

I THANK YOU FOREVER.

Chapter 18
To My Readers

First, I thank you for your interest in buying and reading my book. A large sum of your contributions will help to provide assistance to the needy poor in Cambodia if this book is successful. I know my ideas in this book are strange and unprecedented to the world, and even to my people. I expect that some of you will disagree and dislike what I wrote, but I ask that you please forgive me and allow me to express my freedom. I wrote this book for peaceful purposes only, as I have already mentioned in my preface.

With your voices and Christ over my head, I still strongly believe the wounds, scars, and pain of my unfortunate people can be reduced or eliminated with your help, and the same mistakes will never be repeated. I hope the whole world will keep their eyes on neighboring countries to prevent them from expanding their borders and taking advantage of Cambodia.

Unfortunate Cambodia

Some of you might understand and agree with me regarding the guilty parties who left their fingerprints at the crime scene in Cambodia while sneaking away free, but once again, please do not use this book to direct blame only toward my beloved adopted country, the United States. I have never written anything or read any book in my whole life. Every word and sentence I wrote is in dedication to my suffering people. I broke down so many times during my writing and rereading. This book will remain my first and my last.

Thank you, Christ, you save my life. I am able to speak the truth of the painful memories of my people to the world. Now I will feel free and very happy when it is time for me to leave this world.

You are my judge. Thank you very much. May CHRIST and Buddha bless the free World.

S O L O N G

Christopher Sim

My dear unfortunate fellow Cambodians, we were nearly wiped out by our neighboring countries. The Vietnam War had nearly ended, and yet, the conspiracy of the twentieth century nearly sent us back to the Stone Age. Millions of you had a very violent death. When you cried and asked for help, nobody heard or came to your rescue. Even to this day, the whole world still ignores your pain and suffering. I have spent 29 years walking and delivering mail in the streets of Los Angeles County, and in my spare time, I was finally able to bring all your voices, cries, and tears together to the world court. "my readers and CHRIST" for help. I ask for both to reexamine these past events.

    I thank all my best friends for supporting me. I apologize for only one thing: that I kept my project a secret for almost the entire writing process and hid the contents of this book until the end. Finally, I thank my wife and children for supporting me, even though they could not help me in writing this book. I do not blame them at all. My wife is very sensitive and hurt by the violent past. Her wonderful father exchanged his life for the lives of his nine children and his beloved wife. His name was on the manifest with LON NOL on the way out to freedom, but he chose the ultimate price by swapping his life for the lives of his loved ones.

I have a dream to rebuild one of the churches that was burned down by the Vietminh during the French protectorate if my book becomes a success, not show hatred toward the Vietminh, but in the memory of the French and Cambodian soldiers who shed their blood to protect that resort and that church (Bokor).

I hope and pray for help, but this time from CHRIST.

www.ingramcontent.com/pod-product-compliance
Lightning Source LLC
Chambersburg PA
CBHW070115080526
44586CB00013B/1306